Our Side of
the Playground
What boys think of girls

Our Side of the Playground
What boys think of girls

Compiled by
Tony Bradman

Illustrated by Kim Palmer

RED FOX

A Red Fox Book
Published by Random House Children's Books
20 Vauxhall Bridge Road, London SW1V 2SA

A division of Random House UK Ltd

London Melbourne Sydney Auckland
Johannesburg and agencies throughout the world

First published by the Bodley Head Children's Books 1991

Red Fox edition 1992
Reprinted 1992

Printed and bound in Great Britain by
Cox & Wyman Ltd, Reading, Berkshire

ISBN 0 09 997770 2

Contents

Acknowledgements

The following poems are being published for the first time in this anthology and appear by permission of their authors unless otherwise stated:

Valentine by Michelle Magorian; *Mary Potters* by Peter Dixon; *Poetry Lesson* by Jennifer Curry; *Freak* by Brian Moses; *My Eyes are Watering* by Trevor Harvey; *Boy on the Beach* and *Left Out Together* by Eric Finney; *Stevie Scared* by Richard Edwards; *The Average Boy's Poem* by Malorie Blackman; *The Limpet* and *Looking For a Place* by Janet Greenyer; *Lines for Miss Dalheim* and *Smith's Quiff* by Gina Douthwaite; *I've Got a Valentine* by Allan Frewin; *Hey You!* and *Penny and Kathryn* by Dave Calder; *Girls* by Robert Sparrow; *Georgie Porgie* by John Kitching; *Rosie McAluskey* by Gareth Owen.

The editor and publishers would like to thank the following for permission to use copyright material in this collection:

David Higham Associates for *Girls* by John Cunliffe from *Standing on a Strawberry*, published by Andre Deutsch; Wendy Cope for *Ever So Cute* from *Island of the Children*, published by Orchard Books; Colin McNaughton for *Nice To See The Boys Playing So Well Together* © 1989 Colin McNaughton, taken from *Ten Golden Years*, published in the UK by Walker Books Ltd; Peters, Fraser & Dunlop Group Ltd for *The Unincredible Hulk-in-law* and *I'm a Grown Man Now*, from *Sky in the Pie*, published by Kestrel; Penguin Books Ltd for *A True Story* by Michael Rosen from *You Tell Me* by Roger McGough and Michael Rosen (Kestrel Books 1979), copyright © Michael Rosen 1979; Collins Publishers for *The Pain* by Gareth Owen from *Song of the City*; *Ties* by Brough Girling appears by kind permission of Brough Girling c/o Caroline Sheldon Literary Agency; *Our Side of the Playground* appears by

Our Side of the Playground
What boys think of girls

Freak

Why do I start walking
half in the gutter, half on the kerb,
or wave my arms like a lunatic,
why does everything I say sound absurd?

My voice is always A.W.O.L.
whenever I start to speak,
the words in my mouth are like boulders,
she must think I'm some sort of freak.

Why is it when I take her hand,
mine's all clammy and cold?
She's always calm and confident,
I feel about three years old.

I don't think I'm much to look at,
my hair blows about in the breeze.
I don't want to take her swimming,
I know she'll laugh at my knees.

Mum says it's just a phase
and my gawkiness will pass,
but I really do like her a lot,
more than anyone else in our class.

And thinking about it I can't believe
I've any chance of success
when I ask if I can see her again
but she looks at me and says, 'Yes!'

Brian Moses

Smith's Quiff

Stuck-up Smith coiffed his quiff,
exercised his jaw,

sensing scent, tense he went
at the sight he saw:

gaggled girls, crimson curls,
giggled at the door,

grinned his way, Sharon, Kay.
Smith, he looked once more.

Lashes, black, flashed right back
way across the floor.

Smith perceived, yes, believed
he they fluttered for.

Glossy lips, waggled hips,
cheeks red-radish-raw,

legs from skirts short as shirts
beckoned: 'Je t'adore,'

so Smith thought. (*He'd been caught!*)
What could be in store? . . .

'Hi-ya, Smith. Like your quiff,
's better than before.'

Fingers twitched, eager, itched
Smith's quiff to explore –
ruffled it, scruffled it.
Smith let out a roar!

fled, pell-mell, for his gel
down the corridor

in a tizz, bent on his
image to restore.
Gina Douthwaite

Rosie McAluskey

From a standing start
The two of us
Can race the leccy train
Out of Ainsdale Station
To the first telegraph pole
Where the sandhills begin,
The live line crackles
And smells of lightning.
'One foot on that
And you're nowt
But a pile of smoking ash,'
Rosie tells me, smiling.
'Mr Rimmer's dog ran on it
Last Christmas Eve
And there was nowt to bury.'

She's full of tales like this:
The woman who swallowed a python's egg;
The whale that was thrown up on the beach
With a Ford van in its stomach
And the driver still alive;
The man who cleaned the chimney
And his wife came back
And lit a fire.

We watch a sparrow settle
On the length of steel.
He hops and sings to us
While the murderous voltage
Pours beneath his feet.
My Dad has told me

All there is to know
Of electricity and death.
Sparrows are safe
Because they are not earthed.
'Unless,' says Rosie,
'They have one leg
That's really long!'

We walk down Station Road
Our four eyes skinned
For limping sparrows
With uneven legs.
It's for things like this,
I try to tell the gang,
I walk home
With Rosie McAluskey.

Gareth Owen

Georgie Porgie

Georgie Porgie
Pie and pud
Kissed the girls:
They thought it good.

They never tried to run away,
But begged for more
Both night and day.

John Kitching

Girls

The girls are huddled together,
Keeping all the boys out.
What is it that they can be talking
So earnestly about?

What secrets do they tell one another?
Really, we would like to hear,
But they give us 'the look' and go silent
If we get anywhere near.

Is it they've some special knowledge?
Do they know girl-secret jokes?
Or is the whole thing a big set-up,
Just a deliberate hoax?

If by 'accident' a football
Should interrupt their chatter,
They will pointedly ignore us
As if we didn't matter.

We watch them with some suspicion;
The smiles, laughter, fuss.
Could it be, we sometimes wonder,
They are discussing . . . US?

Robert Sparrow

Girls

We've all sorts of girls in our school:
Bony,
Podgy,
Giggly,
Dodgy,
Sickly smiley,
Shampooed and shiny,
Smelly wellies,
Big and busty,
Dirty dusty;
All sorts . . .
Some pretty ones, too . . .
One or two really nice ones . . .
Well . . . one, just one . . . really special one.
BUT
The one I really hate,
Is Miss Whisper-behind-her-hand.
She gives me a smooth look,
Snooty;
Then she whispers to her Special Friend,
And I know it's something nasty,
. . . about me.

John Cunliffe

Ever So Cute

Little boy dressed in his white judo suit,
Little black belt looking ever so cute.
Hush! Hush! Whisper who dares!
Christopher Robin can throw you downstairs.

Go on Mummy, it's only ten –
I want to watch *Dracula's Bride* again.
It's ever so good when he bites ladies' necks –
Me and my teddy like violence and sex.

And when it's over I want to play
The video game we bought today.
Shooting down spaceships. Bleep, bleep, bleep! Kill, kill!
I'll score three million and Dad will get nil.

Little boy growing so sturdy and tough –
Better not argue or he'll cut up rough.
Hush! Hush! Whatever you say,
Christopher Robin will get his own way.

Wendy Cope

Smoke

They tossed the cigarette butts carelessly away
mimicking wealth or world-weariness, but they'd eyed
each other closely, measuring each drag, each face,
for signs of weakening. And now they all felt slightly sick
and nervous of showing it they talked too hard, too loud.
They kicked the air, the litter. They jostled,
circling and shoving as they left the alleyway.
They moved round each other like dancers on the same small
    stage.
When they saw the girls they whistled for attention,
shouted suggestions. But they were still watching each
other.

Dave Calder

Nice To See The Boys Playing So Well Together

I'll sting you with my tonsilizor,
Sting! Sting!
       I'll blast you into chickenpox,
       Blast! Blast!
I'll zap you into molly cules,
Zap! Zap!
       I'll flatten you with my inter-galactic cruncher,
       Flatten! Flatten!
I'll scrunch you with my monster-bomb,
Scrunch! Scrunch!
       I'll exterminate you with my exterminator-ray,
       Exterminate! Exterminate!
I'll blap you with my meat-seeking missile,
Blap! Blap!
       I'll sock you with my sock-blaster,
       Sock! Sock!
I'll horror you with my sock-blaster,
Horror! Horror!
       I'll wipe you off the face of the planet!
Then I'll wipe you off the face of the galaxy!
       And I'll wipe you off the face of the universe!
Well, I'll, I'll punch you in the nose!

*'Mummy! Mummy! Billy says he's gonna punch me
in the nose!'*

                             Colin McNaughton

The Unincredible Hulk-in-law

Being the Incredible Hulk's
scrawny stepbrother ain't easy.
Sticky-fisted toddlers
Pick fights with me
in misadventure playgrounds.

On beaches
seven-stone weaklings
kick sand in my eyes
vandalize my pies
and thrash me with candyfloss.

They all tell their friends
how they licked the Hulk . . .
(. . . well not the Hulk exactly,
but an incredibly unincredible relative).

Bullied by Brownies
mugged by nuns
without a doubt
the fun's gone out
of having a TV star in the family.

Think I'll marry
Wonderwoman's asthmatic second cousin
and start a commune in Arkansas
for out-of-work, weedy
super heroes-in-law.

Roger McGough

Valentine

She gave me a card with hearts and flowers,
Kisses and a soppy cupid.
Today, she asked me where I lived.
I didn't tell her; I'm not stupid.

Michelle Magorian

I've Got a Valentine

I've got a Valentine.
It hasn't got a name on it.
It says:
> 'Roses are red, violets are blue,
> I am in heaven when I kiss you.'

I've shown it to everyone.
I've never had a Valentine before.
The funny thing is
I don't remember ever kissing any girls.
Perhaps it was delivered to the wrong address.
I hope not.
Perhaps there's a girl out there
Who *dreams* about kissing me.
I wish she'd put her name.
I expect it was only a joke.
But it might not have been.
> 'Roses are red, violets are blue,
> My kisses are waiting, but I don't know for who.'

Allan Frewin

Lines for Miss Dalheim

Miss Dalheim, Miss Dalheim will you be mine?
You can't love old Loo Brush who took you to dine
out at McDonald's. You can't take a shine
to Loo Brush. He's ancient! He's past twenty-nine!

Miss Dalheim, Miss Dalheim will you be mine?
I'll buy you a meal at a restaurant, *with wine*.
You won't have to queue, with the kids, in a line.
Could we, Miss Dalheim? Oh, could we combine?

Miss Dalheim, Miss Dalheim will you be mine?
My car-washing money will go up in time.
I'm selling my *Walkman*. Please wait or I'll pine.
(Don't bristle – but Brush is in sweeping decline.)

Gina Douthwaite

Poetry Lesson

Our teacher says that poets tell us what life's all about.
  (Melissa Bell's a new girl and she sits in front of me.)

Our teacher says that poets paint us pictures with their verse.
  (Melissa Bell has little ears that look like pink sea shells.)

Our teacher says that poets make us look, and think, and see.
  (Melissa Bell has coal-black hair that's just like my cat, Tosh.)

Our teacher says that poets like to touch and taste and sniff.
  (Melissa Bell has an apple-y smell – she gets that stuff from Boots

Our teacher says that poets like to write their thoughts in lines.
  (Melissa Bell, I think you're great, with love from Matty Lee.)
                                        Jennifer Curry

Stevie Scared

Stevie Scared, scared of the dark,
Scared of rats, of dogs that bark,
Scared of his fat dad, scared of his mother,
Scared of his sis and his tattoed brother,
Scared of tall girls, scared of boys,
Scared of ghosts and sudden noise,
Scared of spiders, scared of bees,
Scared of standing under trees,
Scared of shadows, scared of adders,
Scared of the devil, scared of ladders,
Scared of hailstones, scared of rain,
Scared of falling down the drain,
Stevie Scared, scared of showing
He's so scared and people knowing,
Spends his whole time kicking, fighting,
Shoving, pinching, butting, biting,
Bashing little kids about,
(Just in case they find him out).

Richard Edwards

Mary Potters

I love Mary Potters
The best girl in our class,
The girl I want to marry
Though I know that makes you laugh.
I know you think I'm stupid
I know you think girls daft
And when I told big Dawkins . . .
                he laughed
                      and laughed
                              and laughed.
He laughed and said, 'Play footer!
Don't go out with girls
Go and get your skateboard
And spin some danger-whirls.
Go and get your trackbike
I'll race you round the park
We'll pull a ton of wheelies
And get up to a lark . . .

26

We'll go and catch some gudgeon
Or call for Porky Day –
Wrestle with his brother
Or go see Barry Gray . . .
There's tons of things to do mate,
So stick around with us
Me and Mogsy Walters,
Dingo, Dan and Duff.
They'll laugh if you're not there mate,
Gone kissin' girls, I'll say.
So go and get your boots on
. . . It's goals

                 not

girls

            – today!

But –
       but I like Mary Potters
Her smile
Her punky hair
The way she holds her pencil
The way she doesn't care.
I've never spoken to her
– But I'm going to do it soon
Walk her back to her house
One day –

         or afternoon . . .

She's really really smashing
And I've got to find a way
To put my arm around her
At dinnertime one day.
I think I'll try tomorrow
Or Tuesday after school
Or Friday after swimming
Outside the swimming pool.
I might just wait till next term
Or in the wintertime
. . . The Christmas party's coming –
Yes, Christmas will be fine.
      Perhaps I'll wait till next year
      Hallowe'en perhaps –
        when I'm not quite so busy
      Playing with the chaps.
So off to play the big match
Off with Dawkins' lads
Gloves and cap and tracksuit
– My special goalie pads.
      Special kinds of goal kicks
      Super diving dives
      – Wait till Dawkins sees me
      – Wait till he arrives.

WHAT!!!!!!

Dawkins isn't coming!!!!!!

You saw him with a girl!!!!!!

– a sort of punky hairdo
an ear – with just one pearl?

A girl called Mary Potters . . .
    And Dawkins by her side
    Holding hands in Safeways
    And trying hard to hide!!!!!!

Dawkins – you're a rotter
Potters' potty too
Holding hands in Safeways
– a stupid thing to do.
Oh come and play some footer
With Spud and Mick and me
I'm dreaming super soccer
   . . . (and Mary on my knee).

Peter Dixon

The Limpet

She watches while we play football,
The boys wave her away.
She folds her arms determinedly,
I know she's here to stay.

They've nicknamed her 'The Limpet'
And say it's me she likes.
It makes me feel embarrassed
As we circle with our bikes.

It's then that I draw close to her –
Will she think me rather tame?
And does she know that when she's there
I play a better game?

Janet Greenyer

Looking for a Place

On our side of the playground
We're hardly ever still;
Boys run and shout, or joke about
Then, turning, kick a ball.

On their side of the playground
Girls treat us with disdain;
They skip with ropes, or talk a bit –
I find them quite a pain.

But in the middle of the playground
I'm looking for a place
Where I can think and dream a bit
Without a loss of face.

Janet Greenyer

The Pain

Coming home from school when I was seven
I told my mother of the pain.
'Where is the pain?' she asked.
'Here,' I said, holding before me
Two imaginary pillows in the air.
'Where were you when it started?'
'At Farnborough Road Juniors
But then I took it on the bus with me.'
'At what time did the pain start?'

'Between the end of dinnertime
And the ringing of the bell for afternoon.'
'Was it something you ate? How did you notice it?'
'It walked through the door of Miss Mellor's class.
Before there was just me
Afterwards there were two of us,
The pain and me.'
'Was anything said? Did anybody notice?'
'Something was said about the register.
When the room was empty
The pain had made its home there.'
'Can't you tell me more?' my mother said.
She was getting bored with the conversation.
'What would you call the pain?'
'The pain is called Nancy Muriel Oliver
And is pale with yellow hair.
Is there nothing you can do,
Nothing you can say?'
'No,' said my mother,
Closing the medicine cabinet.
'Just go back to school tomorrow
And pray it never goes away.'

Gareth Owen

Left Out Together

There's the crowd of them again,
The boys with their girls,
Carefree,
Laughing and chatting and going somewhere –
Not including me.
They never say,
'Why don't you come too?'
I wander away
And pretend I don't care –
But I do.
And when they come back
They've got it all to remember
And share.
I wouldn't know:
I wasn't there.

I tried once to be friends with a girl;
Well, actually, I've tried twice.
But – this is the truth –
I've always thought
That you looked quiet and nice.
You look as though
You might be feeling the same:
Left on the sidelines,
Out of the game . . .?
You are?
I was actually wondering whether
We could team up and both be
Left out together.

Eric Finney

Later the Same Day

Later the same day
I felt my tooth.
It hurt. It was loose.
Why did she hit me?

We were throwing stones
Into a puddle
On our side of the playground,
Trying to wet everybody.

Julie and her mates
Came over.
I said, 'Julie, be careful,
You'll get wet.'

Jason laughed
And splashed water
All over her shoes.

I hit him for that.

Julie glared at me.
Later, without warning
She smacked me hard
On the head.

'That's for hitting Jason,'
She said.

'But he splashed water over you.'

'So what?' she said.
'I wanted him to.'

Philip Ennis

34

My Eyes Are Watering

I've got a cold
And that is why
My eyes are watering.

It's nothing to do
With getting caught
When I had planned
To SMASH
The rounders ball
SO FAR
That it would go
Into PERMANENT ORBIT
Round the school.
It would've done, too –
If Lucy Smith
Hadn't RUSHED
To catch it.

'Look at Trevor –
He's having a cry!'
Not true.
I've got a cold
And THAT is why
My eyes are watering.

O.K.?

Trevor Harvey

A True Story

First love
when I was ten.

We planned a trip
up to town
Quite a grand thing to do
Up to town
The long ride on the train
all the way
up to town.

The day before our trip
up to town
She said, 'Do you mind if Helen
comes with us
up to town?'
'Great,' I said,
'all three of us, we'll all go
on the train
up to town.'

So that's how it was –
all three of us,
her, Helen and me,
going on our trip
up to town.

But when we got
up to town,
all three of us –
her, Helen and me,

there was this long tunnel
and her friend, Helen,
goes and says:
'Hey – let's run away from him.'
And that's what they did.

So then there wasn't
all three of us any more.
There was just me,
standing in the tunnel.
I didn't chase after them.
I went home.

Michael Rosen

Wishes

Oh, if you were a little boy,
      And I was a little girl –
Why, you would have some whiskers grow
      And then my hair would curl.

Ah! if I could have whiskers grow,
      I'd let you have my curls;
But what's the use of wishing it –
      Boys never can be girls.

Kate Greenaway

Ties

At our school
All us boys
Tie our ties
With the short end

SHORT

And the long thin end as

LONG AND THIN AS WE CAN MAKE
    THEM

We don't do it to please the girls
We don't do it to annoy the teachers

We all just do it to be different.
We all do.

Brough Girling

Hey You!

Hey you, we're the boys at the back of the class:
look at us, we're great cos we say we are;
thinking's too soft when you want to scrap
when you've got to talk big
when you've got to act hard
and sitting down's a kind of trap
when you need to mess
when you need to act:

and we know we're boss cos everything stops,
the girls can't work, the smart act dumb,
when we're shouting loud and kicking mad:
for writing's boring
fighting's fun,
we're big because we're bad;
we think we're great
and we're never wrong,
we're ace star brill the lot
and we can't wait till the bell has rung:
we're only here cos we had to come.

Dave Calder

I'm a Grown Man Now

I'm a grown man now
Don't easily scare
(if you don't believe me
ask my teddy bear).

Roger McGough

Penny and Kathryn

Penny and Kathryn
that year they seemed older
though we were all ten.
I'd watch them in class,
they didn't chatter or laugh,
were so calm at their work
it made me feel nervous.
Gawky Penny now seemed
slim and clever, her new glasses
made her eyes large and dreamy
above the small pout of her mouth.
Kathryn was stocky, strong,
her thick hair shook as she moved
always as if sure where she was going:
I liked that energy, almost feared it.

I wasn't mooning over them, they were just
more interesting than the other girls,
somehow stronger than the boys.
I would have liked to be friends with them.

But one warm evening, going home,
we saw them behind us on the road,
two other boys and me, we said
let's hide, let's jump out, it's fun –
we thought it friendly, meant no harm.
And I hid behind a gatepost like the others,
enjoying the wait, the tension,
and leapt up grinning, happy as a puppy,

but the girls didn't look surprised
or laugh or run or anything:

they just looked, and the looks
said they were past that sort of game,
that we were silly little boys, to be ignored,
and they left me standing foolish by the wall
feeling they were right and knowing
even as I made a rude face to cover up my shame
how big a gap there was between us
that I couldn't cross until I learnt
what different games would please them.

Dave Calder

The Average Boy's Poem

I'm just a kid – I have to fight,
Even though it isn't right.
I have to pull my sister's hair
And make believe that I don't care.
Put spiders down my girlfriend's dress,
Whilst teachers, talking, slam my desk.
Play football when I'd rather read,
Stay silent when I fall and bleed.
Chuck food around the cafeteria
Until the girls all have hysteria.
Laugh at cissy poetry,
(Although I like it secretly).
Skipping? That's a total no!
Despite the fact I'd love a go.
Instead of talking, I must shout,
To make sure that the words come out.

My mum said that it gave her joy,
When I was born and was a boy,
But seems to me, down deep inside
That girls – they don't pretend or hide
The way I do when not alone . . .
And yet I hate it on my own.
When I grow up then I will do
The things I've always wanted to.
I'll dance around and be athletic
Without friends saying I'm pathetic.
(They don't say that when Michael Jackson
Is the centre of attraction.)
And for myself I'll wash and cook
And not hide when I read a book.
My girl and I will go out walking,
Holding hands and really talking.
And as we stroll along the street
It just won't matter who we meet.
When I am older, I won't care
How many people stop and stare.
I'll do the things I never did
Because right now I'm just a kid.

Malorie Blackman

Boys Will Be Boys

Look at little Peter. Isn't he a terror?
Shooting all the neighbours with his cowboy gun.
Screaming like a jet plane. Always throwing something.
I just can't control him. Trouble – he's the one.

Ah, but boys will be boys, it's a fact of human nature,
And girls will grow up to be mothers.

Look at little Janie. Doesn't she look pretty?
Playing with her dollies. Proper little mum.
Never getting dirty, never being naughty –
Don't punch your sister, Peter! Now look what you've
    done!

Ah, but boys will be boys, it's a fact of human nature,
And girls will grow up to be mothers.

What's come over Janie? Janie's turning nasty.
Left hook to the body. Right hook in the eye.
Vicious little hussy. Now Peter's started bawling.
What a bloody cissy! Who said you could cry?

Because boys must be boys, it's a fact of human nature,
And girls must grow up to be mothers.

Now things are topsy-turvy. Janie wants a football.
Peter just seems happy pushing prams along.
Makes you feel so guilty. Kids are such a worry.
Doctor, doctor, tell me, Where did we go wrong?

Because boys must be boys, it's a fact of human nature,
And girls must grow up to be mothers.

Leon Rosselson

My Little Brother

My mother had a baby.
And my friends were quick to say,
'That's the end of all your fun –
You won't forget this day.'

They said he'd be a nuisance,
He'd be a smelly pest,
He'd tire out my mum and dad . . .
Oh, I forget the rest.

It's turned out very different;
It wasn't lots of bother.
In fact, the truth is simple:
I like my little brother.

He's lots of fun to play with,
He crawls about and smiles.
I like to take him to the park
And push him round for miles.

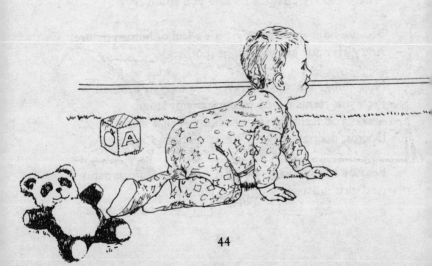

My parents do look tired,
But I haven't been ignored,
And though we're very busy,
We're never, ever bored.

My friends all think I'm stupid,
That something's wrong with me;
Boys don't like babies, they all say.
Well, I think differently.

I don't care what my friends think,
Or say to one another;
I'm glad Mum had our baby –
I *like* my little brother.

Tony Bradman

A Boy's Song

Where the pools are bright and deep,
Where the grey trout lies asleep
Up the river and o'er the lea,
That's the way for Billy and me.

Where the blackbird sings the latest,
Where the hawthorn blooms the sweetest,
Where the nestlings chirp and flee,
That's the way for Billy and me.

Where the mowers mow the cleanest,
Where the hay lies thick and greenest;
There to trace the homeward bee,
That's the way for Billy and me.

Where the hazel bank is steepest,
Where the shadow falls the deepest,
Where the clustering nuts fall free,
That's the way for Billy and me.

Why the boys should drive away
Little sweet maidens from their play,
Or love to banter and fight so well,
That's the thing I never could tell.

But this I know, I love to play
Through the meadow, among the hay;
Up the water and o'er the lea,
That's the way for Billy and me.

James Hogg

Boy on the Beach

Walking the dunes
Behind the strand,
I saw a boy alone
On wide, wet sand.
A stillness held him
As he faced the tide,
Slowly raised his arms
Then spread them wide;
Stayed so for a minute
Then breaking the spell,
Wrote large on the sand
With a stone or shell.
Walking on through marram grass
I soon could see:
He'd simply written
I AM ME.

Eric Finney

Our Side of
the Playground
What girls think of boys

Our Side of
the Playground
What girls think of boys

Compiled by
Tony Bradman

Illustrated by Kim Palmer

RED FOX

A Red Fox Book
Published by Random House Children's Books
20 Vauxhall Bridge Road, London SW1V 2SA

A division of Random House UK Ltd

London Melbourne Sydney Auckland
Johannesburg and agencies throughout the world

First published by the Bodley Head Children's Books 1991

Red Fox edition 1992
Reprinted 1992

Printed and bound in Great Britain by
Cox & Wyman Ltd, Reading, Berkshire

ISBN 0 09 997770 2

Contents

What Girls Think of Boys

Acknowledgements

The following poems are being published for the first time in this anthology and appear by permission of their authors unless otherwise stated:

Wrong by Brian Morse; *Neighbours* by Hazel Townson; *There Were These Two Girls* by Dave Ward; *Aliens* by Moira Andrew; *First Kiss* by Alan Bold; *The Boy I'd Love* by Bernard Young; *Wash Up the Dishes* and *The Show-off Girl* by Lorraine Simeon; *He Loves Me . . .* and *Disco Nite* by Wes Magee; *Bully for You* and *Kiss Chase, Fish Face* by Ian Souter; *A Touch of Class* by John Kitching; *What's Best* by June Crebbin; *Kissing Games* by Eileen Round; *One Girl to Nil* by Gina Douthwaite; *Horrible Hannah* by Jean Ure; *Little Miss Muffet* by Dave Calder; *Here Come the Third-years* by Tony Bradman.

The editor and publishers would like to thank the following for permission to use copyright material in this collection:

Cadbury's National Exhibition of Children's Art – Poetry Section for *Boys Are . . .* by Marie Neeson and *Lessons* by Lorraine Grant; Farrar, Straus and Giroux, Inc for *Mattie Lou at Twelve* from *Spin a Soft Black Song* by Nikki Giovanni; copyright © 1971, 1985 by Nikki Giovanni, reprinted by permission of Farrar, Straus and Giroux, Inc; Holt, Rinehart and Winston Publishers for *Queenie* by Leland B. Jacobs from *Alphabet of Girls*; *Who Is De Girl?* by John Agard by kind permission of John Agard, c/o Caroline Sheldon Literary Agency; *Lyn ♡ Donnie!* by Gina Wilson by kind permission of Gina Wilson, c/o Gina Pollinger Literary Agency; Irene Rawnsley for *Good Girls*, first published in *Toughie Toffee*, published by Collins, 1989; Dave Calder for *Little Miss Muffet*, first published in *Bamboozled* by Other 1987; Collins Publishers for *Would You Believe It?* by Mick Gowar from *Swings and Round-*

Our Side of
the Playground
What girls think of boys

The Boy I'd Love

The boy I'd love
    To sit near?

The boy I'd like
    To tease?

The boy I'd share
    My lunch with?

The boy I'd choose
    To please?

His name
    Is not John Roberts

His name
    Is not Tim Smith

His name
    Is not James Richards

His name
    Is not Tom Swift

The boy I'd love
    To sit near

The boy I'd choose
    To please

Teaches us
    Mathematics

His name
    Is Henry C.

T. Maguire
    (Esquire)
Bernard Young

A Touch of Class

When Miss asks a question,
If you're a girl in the class
There's no point in putting your hand up,
Not worth bothering to stand up.
Might as well bring a big brass band up!

Some boy will just call out
Or boorishly bawl out,
Or spray the atomic fall-out
Of his unthought answer – right or wrong.
A girl may sit with her hand up
All day long
       But Miss
Will take not the slightest notice.
John Kitching

Horrible Hannah

Hannah S. Hancock
Is the
Most hateful girl that I know.

She is just
S
   o
     o
       o
         o
Obnoxious.

I can't stand her.

There was a time
We were best mates,
Her and me.
Did everything together.

      Sat together
      Walked together
      Played together
      Ate together.

Everything.

Then she spat in my face
And I hate her.

What happened, you see,
Was I got this crush
On Christopher Bigg

And he
Got this crush on me.
We'd gone out together the once,
And were going to go out again,
And next time for sure he'd have kissed me,
I know that he would,
But *then* . . .

What do you think?

Ms Hannah Hancock,
Her that calls herself
My best mate,
This person that I now *hate*,
On account of she is so unspeakably
Evil,
She comes up to me next day
All gloating
And she goes,
'Guess what?'
She goes.
'I went for a walk in the Park last night,
With Christopher Bigg,' she goes.
'He held my hand and he kissed me,
Right on the lips,'
She goes.
And at first I didn't believe her,
But then I knew it was true.
And I called her a cheating cow
And she said that I was just jealous,
''Cos he likes me better than you.'

And then I used bad language,
And she used even worse.

And I tore at her hair
And I scratched her,
And she kicked me on the shin.
And I threatened to punch her teeth in
If she went out with Chris again.
And she said she'd do just what she wanted,
'You hideous horrible thing!'

And she put up two fingers
And made a rude sign
And spat in my face
And I hate her.

****

PS

Just yesterday I heard
That Hannah's been given the elbow.
Poor Hannah
I feel
S
   o
      o
         o
            o
Sorry for her.

Christopher Bigg has dropped her.
He's going with Rosemary Mitchell.
So maybe
Just maybe
Possibly,
Maybe,

Hannah and me
Will be friends again.
Maybe.

You can't trust boys,
They're *fickle*.

Jean Ure

One Girl to Nil

Zipper Zach zoomed up the pitch,
drew up sharply with a stitch,
disappeared under a scrum.
Scarce of air he went quite numb.

To the rescue came young Zeph
like the west wind, from the left,
wafted on in borrowed kit,
burst the blighters like a zit:

studded boots mashed blood with mud,
heads met others with a thud.
Zephyr sent their senses crashing,
scored a winner bully bashing,

dribbled off towards the goal
wobbling like a new-born foal,
wumphed the ball – her final kill.
Zach's team won: one girl to nil.

Gina Douthwaite

What's Best

Funny how it's all right for me
To play soccer but not all right
For David to join in girls' games.
People keep saying 'We saw you last night
With your boyfriend.' When I ignore them
They say: 'Has he kissed you?
Do you love him?'
I wish they'd leave us alone.

We like the same things. We invent
The same games. We've been friends
Ever since we both wanted the same book
In the library three years ago
And the teacher said we could share. We
Did a whole project on it. We like being together.
'When are you getting married?' people say.
I wish they'd leave us alone.

Next year they've put us in different classes,
People say it's for the best. My Mum says:
'You'll be able to make friends with girls now.'
But we'll see each other at playtimes
And dinnertimes and after school and weekends.
Funny how other people always think
They know what's best.
Why can't they leave us alone?

June Crebbin

Little Miss Muffet

Little Miss Muffet
sat on her tuffet
eating her butties with Bert.

A spider crawled on her hand:
she picked it up and
shoved it straight down the back of his shirt.

Dave Calder

Lynn ♡ Donnie!

All the girls in Standard Six
Have got Valentine cards galore,
Except for me. I've just got one
– And mine's from *Donnie McGraw*!

Donnie McGraw can't see too well,
And he's microscopically small,
And sometimes the whole of a day goes by
And he doesn't talk at all.

And nobody ever goes home with him,
They think his mum's so mean –
On Sundays she makes him wear a kilt
To keep his trousers clean.

She feeds him broth and turnip-tops
And watery fish, half-raw;
They shout: '*Hey, Lynn! If you want to get thin,
Move in with Mrs McGraw!*'

But, when Donnie's alone (it's a secret, this;
I'm the only one to know),
He gets Uncle Hector's bagpipes out
And treats himself to a blow . . .

Then, he's marching down the heather track,
And through the misty glen,
With a swirl of plaid and a skirl of pipes
And a thousand fighting men . . .

But, in Standard Six, he's 'Haggis Face',
'MacMuck', and 'Spotty Jock'!
And some of them take his accent off . . .
Well, they're in for an awful shock

– Because I'm in love with Donnie McGraw
And his card on Valentine's Day!
He's the first and only boy in the world
Who thinks that *I'm OK*!

Gina Wilson

Good Girls

Good girls
will always go like clockwork
home from school,

through the iron gates
where clambering boys
whisper and pull,

past houses
where curtains twitch
and a fingery witch beckons,

by the graveyard
where stone angels stir,
itching their wings,

past tunnelled woods
where forgotten wolves wait
for prey,

past dens
and caves and darknesses
they go like clockwork;

and when they come
to school again
their homework's done.

Irene Rawnsley

Wash Up the Dishes

'Wash up the dishes,' my mum says.
Well you should see the state of the pots!
You would think I was a chambermaid
For all the thanks I got.

'Make your brother some toast and jam,
Hurry, do bring the washing in.'
All I wanted to do was watch *Neighbours*
But my hopes are growing thin.

In comes my dad; 'My feet are so sore,
Please make me a strong cup of tea.'
Well I've had gymnastics, science and maths
But does anyone care about me?

'Have you seen my trainers? I'm going to be late,
I'm meeting Amanda at nine.'
My brother does nothing but eat, sleep, and date.
When he wants to go out, that's fine.

When I want to go out, it's 'Be in by ten,
Where are you going, with who?'
I'd say I deserve some more freedom and trust
After all the work that I do.

When I am eighteen I'm going to move out,
I'll get my own flat, wait and see.
I've six years to go, and one thing I know
Is, they'll never survive without ME.

Lorraine Simeon

Boys Are . . .

Something to lie awake about thinking of,
Boys are.
Something to admire,
To watch from afar,
Boys are.
Something to sing about,
To get nervous about,
To bite nails out about,
Boys are.
Something to feel sorry for,
To adore,
Or simply feel are a bore,
Boys are.
Something to write home about,
To let your heart ring out,
To murmur 'Yuk' about,
Boys are.
Dynamite,
Delectable,
Different,
Maybe dull,
Wide range,
Wonderful,
Worth it?
Boys . . .

Marie Neeson

Aliens

Boys were a foreign breed
to me, one of two sisters
at an all-girl school.

Charlie lived two doors
down. He had crinkly fair
hair, owl-like spectacles.

He was my passport to
finding out what boys were
about, so I spied on him.

I'd follow him along the
lane, hide behind bushes.
He wheezed as he breathed.

Asthma, I know now, but
I thought boys were like
that. He walked head-down.

Charlie's mother shouted
a lot. 'Charles!' she'd
yell. 'Come along, lad!'

He'd mumble in reply, but
didn't hurry. The back door
would close behind him.

They led a mysterious
dark-curtained life,
Charlie and his parents.

I didn't think they
knew I existed. Charlie
never smiled, never said 'Hi!'

Not until the day my bag
broke. Books and papers
spilled across the pavement.

'Let me help,' Charlie said.
He picked up stuff, gutter-
wet, bundled it into my arms.

He smiled. 'I've seen you
around,' he said. 'But I never
know what to say to girls.'

So that was it. I was an
alien too. His mother
watched us from the window.

'CHARLES!' she called.
'I'd better go,' he said.
He waved and went inside.

Moira Andrew

Kissing Games

Parents shouldn't bring up children
Their world isn't ours
When I come from school and kiss her
Mum just stands and glowers;

Says I must be after something
Trouble is – she's right
There's this vital boy/girl party
On next Saturday night.

I know this boy who's going to it
I like him quite a lot
– Big mistake to mention him though
Mum says, 'Definitely NOT.'

I say I've matured since last time
And don't plan to be a nun.
'Well, no more kissing games my girl!'
'Oh, Mum! It's only fun.'

I grovel then and try to please her
Even say I'll clean my room;
She says she'd jump over Pluto
If I did, not just the Moon!

All my brilliant reasoning then
My Mum never hears
When she thinks she's won the case
She just removes her ears;

Declared she played no kissing games
Till she was twenty-three!
She must have found it boring
Arranging to have me.

Eileen Round

This poem was inspired by a story written for her
school magazine by Rebecca Mason of
Hinchingbrooke School, Huntingdon.

There Were These Two Girls

There were these two girls
strutting down the street
whistling
loud enough to crack the windows

they were whistling
at the moon
but the moon just winked
as it hid behind a cloud

they were whistling
at the lamp-posts
but the lamp-posts just blinked
as they leaned together
like drunks

they were whistling
at the boys
who slinked off round the corner
like shamefaced puppies
with their tails between their legs

they were whistling
at the world
then they stood there listening
to see
if the world would whistle back

Dave Ward

Neighbours

I don't want to sit next to Neil.
  If I do, I shall feel such a fool.
Our names will end up in the same silly heart
  And be doodled all over the school.

So I go to Miss Moss and I say,
  'Miss, I don't want to sit next to Neil.'
But she snaps, 'If you make a big thing out of this
  'How d'you think the poor lad's going to feel?'

So I sit where she tells me to sit,
  And I blush as I sink to my chair,
Because Neil has leaped up with a horrified cry:–
  'Miss, I don't want to sit next to Claire!'

Hazel Townson

The Show-off Girl

The show-off girl comes to school every day
Dressed in fashions which make her look cool
She changes her shoes at least twice a day
But I wish she would simply change schools

She does not walk normally like you and me
Her footsteps are tiny and graceful
As for friends, she has two, but I cannot tell why
Her jokes are so old and distasteful

Her hair is so neat, every strand kept in place
With a hair-band she bought in Vienna
She was there for a week, but if I had a choice
Planet Mars is where I'd like to send her

Sometimes I imagine we get in a fight
Though I know that she can't really hurt me
I won't hurt her either, I'd just like to make
Her so-fashionable clothes nice and dirty.

Lorraine Simeon

Kiss Chase, Fish Face

Kiss chase, kiss chase,
Catch them in a lips race.
Kiss chase, kiss chase,
Suck them in the right place.
Kiss chase, kiss chase,
Lips smacking their face.
Kiss chase, kiss chase
Hunt them with a fish face.
Kiss chase, kiss chase,
Grab a gorgeous creature.
Kiss chase, kiss chase,
Make sure it's not your TEACHER!

Ian Souter

Who Is De Girl?

Who is de girl dat kick de ball
then jump for it over de wall

sallyann is a girl so full-o zest
sallyann is a girl dat just can't rest

who is de girl dat pull de hair
of de bully and make him scare

sallyann is a girl so full-o zest
sallyann is a girl dat just can't rest

who is de girl dat bruise she knee
when she fall from de mango tree

sallyann is a girl so full-o zest
sallyann is a girl dat just can't rest

who is de girl dat set de pace
when boys and girls dem start to race

sallyann is a girl so full-o zest
sallyann is a girl dat just can't rest

John Agard

Lessons

I saw you in the street today.
You at your bus-stop,
Me at mine.
Facing each other.
Separated by a small stretch of tarmac.
Or was it more than that?
Memories of the childish pranks
Encouraged by your bets and dares.
We led you on,
Yet you led us.
I never knew which
For sure.
Our eyes met at last
Amidst the crowd.
I wait for recognition.
I saw you in the street today.
You did not know me.

Lorraine Grant

Would You Believe It?

– Jacky's going out with Peter –
– Which one? NOT the one with spots –
– No of course not, Peter Davis –
– Don't believe you
            how d'you know? –
– Tracy told me but you mustn't say
I said so –
                – course not
how did she find out? –
– Well,
Philippa, that's Tracey's mate the one in 3G
her mate Mandy's sister Carol's
best friend Susan and her boyfriend
(his name's Peter)
saw them
            Coming Out The Pictures

(But you mustn't tell A SOUL
cos Jacky's also going out
with someone else as well . . .)

Mick Gowar

Wrong

Martin Cooper tricked me.
He said teacher had gone.
He said, 'Throw it! Go on!'
But she hadn't.
She was just bending down.

'Who threw that?' Miss Dixon shouted.
'That nearly hit me!
What naughty boy did it?
Own up! Own up!'

No one owned up.
We stayed in at play.
We stayed in all day.
But why should I own up?
I'm no boy.

Brian Morse

Round Our Table

Round our table
Sam is in love
With Anthea

But Anthea
Is in love
With Clint

Clint is
Almost in love
With Tracey

But doesn't
Really like
Her squint

That just
Leaves me
And I'm

In a bit
Of a jam
I sit next

To Anthea
And I'm (choke,
Sob, howl)

In love
With
Sam

Tony Bradman

There Was a Little Girl

There was a little girl,
And she had a little curl
    Right in the middle of her forehead.
When she was good
She was very, very good,
    And when she was bad she was horrid.

One day she went upstairs,
When her parents, unawares,
    In the kitchen were occupied with meals
And she stood upon her head
In her little trundle-bed,
    And then began hooraying with her heels.

Her mother heard the noise,
And she thought it was the boys
    A-playing at a combat in the attic;
But when she climbed the stair,
And found Jemima there,
    She took and she did spank her most emphatic.

Henry Wadsworth Longfellow

Mattie Lou at Twelve

they always said 'what a pretty little girl you are'
and she would smile

they always said 'how nice of you to help
your mother with your brothers and sisters'
and she would smile and think

they said 'what lovely pigtails you have
and you plaited them all by yourself!'
and she would say 'thank you'

and they always said 'all those Bs
what a good student you are'
and she would smile and say 'thank you'

they said 'you will make a fine woman some day'
and she would smile and go her way

because she knew

Nikki Giovanni

40

Queenie

Queenie's strong and Queenie's tall.
You should see her bat a ball,
Ride a bike or climb a wall.
(Queenie's not her name at all.)

Queenie's nimble, Queenie's quick.
You should see her throw a stick,
Watch her saw a board that's thick,
See her do her tumbling trick.

Queenie's not afraid, like me,
Of snakes or climbing up a tree.
(I think that's why the boys agree
Queenie's what her name should be.)

Leland B. Jacobs

Disco Nite

Seven p.m. Thursday

In the girls' cloaks
the air gasps with *Nightfall* and *Moonwind*.
The excitement is intense.
Everyone uses the
strawberry flavoured lip gloss
passed round by Philippa Spence.

In a giggling gaggle
the girls rush to the school hall
where the floor shines like a skating rink.
Loud music throbs and pounds.
The disco lights dazzle with flashes
of red, mauve, yellow, green and pink.

And *he's* there,
Dean Moffat in a big stripy shirt
and with gel on his spiky hair.
When the deejay yells,
'Go grab 'em, girls!'
Lisa drags him, protesting, off his chair.

Eight fifty a.m. Friday

Lisa is at the centre
of a playground huddle of girls.
'What happened?' 'Tell us!' 'Own up!'
'I think he loves me,' says Lisa.
She smiles to herself. *'I bet
he marries me when we're grown up.'*

Wes Magee

He Loves Me . . .

> He loves me
> he loves me not
> he loves me
> he loves me not . . .

It's hot, sweltering, as children
spill from the school at lunchtime
and spread across the field.
　　Friday. Fry-day. Sun-high noon.
Today is the thirtieth day
　　of heat-wave June.

Legs splayed wide
three girls sit and pick daisies.
They must endure Sports Day heats
    all that long, hot afternoon.
For them the summer holidays
    can't arrive too soon.

                He loves me
                he loves me not
                he loves me
                he loves me not . . .

It's a massacre.
Daisies by the score
lie beside the girls,
    dying in the sun-stunned air.
The sky's albino eye is unblinking.
    A fierce, fixing glare.

The girls chant lazily,
dreaming who'll be the one
to get lucky with Richard,
    the boy with flame-red hair.
Will it be Francesca or Vikki
    or Claire?

          He loves me
          he loves me not
          he loves me
          he loves me not . . .
                        Wes Magee

      First Kiss

      A rush
      A race
      A hush
      A face:
      A face
      A hush
      A race
      A rush
      Alan Bold

Here Come the Third Years

Here come the third years
Walking arm in arm
Talking about boyfriends
Parading all their charm

Emma's got her hair up
Andrea's got a ring
Charlotte's wearing lipstick
Hear the boys all sing:

Oh you are so beautiful
Be my own true love
I'll give you lots of money
And call you turtle dove

Now listen to the girls sing
They're laughing at the boys . . .
Ooooh! You're all so *ugly*!
And you're making too much noise!

There go the third years
And the boys all shout
They're sticking out their tongues now
And O-U-T spells . . . OUT!

Tony Bradman

Bully For You!

'I'm glad, REALLY GLAD, I'm not (urrr) YOU!
In fact everybody in this playground.
will be REALLY GLAD, they're not (urrr) YOU!
Come to think of it,
everybody in the entire universe
will be REALLY GLAD, they're not (urrr) YOU!
Because when I've finished, done with, got through,
YOU aren't going to recognize,
WHO? – Yes (urrr) – YOU!'

'Who, ME?
This little slip of a ME!
This little puff of a, snuff of a, not enough of a ME!
This little won't hurt a flea, never mind a pea, ME!
YOU ARE THREATENING ME!
Well, BULLY BOY,
I'm not one for much talking or squawking,
so listen very carefully,
for I'M BREATHING DANGER HERE!
Your name may be BULLY BOY
but mine's BULLY GIRL
SO WATCHA!'

Ian Souter

47

Our Side of the Playground

Our side of the playground
Starts right here
So boys can stay away from it
Just keep clear

Our side is wide!

Our side of the playground
Starts here too
And any girl who comes our side
Will end up down our loo

Our side is long!

Our side is tough!

Our side of the playground
Has got a blackbird's nest
It's also good for roller-skates
Which makes our side the best

Our side is strong!

We've got the goalposts!

We've got the net!

Well, we've got paths to skid on ice
And steps for look-out towers
From which we see that your side's nice —
But not as nice as ours!

We've got the football!

Yeah! You wanna bet?

We've got the window
To look into Form Three
Where during break, Mr Hake,
Plays kiss chase with Ms Snee

Our side of the playground!
Our side of the playground!
OUR SIDE OF THE PLAYGROUND!
OUR SIDE OF THE PLAYGROUND!

Well, *we've* got the potting shed
All dark and damp and murky
For keeping toads and secret codes
And spies with dreaded lurgy

If you don't say that our side's best
I'll sock you with my fist!

Just a second . . .

If you do that, I'll yank your plait,
And Chinese-burn your wrist!

By the way . . .
Now we've stopped . . .

We're the best!

OK!

We're the best!

D'you wanna swap?

US! US! US!

Lisa Taylor

49